A RAISIN
IN THE SUN

Lorraine Hansberry

SPARK PUBLISHING

SPARKNOTES is a registered trademark of SparkNotes LLC

Spark Publishing
A Division of Barnes & Noble
120 Fifth Avenue
New York, NY 10011
www.sparknotes.com

ISBN-13: 978-1-4114-0722-0
ISBN-10: 1-4114-0722-9

Please submit changes or report errors to www.sparknotes.com/errors.

Printed in the United States

10 9 8 7 6 5 4 3 2 1

CONTENTS

CONTEXT

L ORRAINE HANSBERRY WAS BORN in Chicago on May 19, 1930, the youngest of four children. Her parents were well-educated, successful black citizens who publicly fought discrimination against black people. When Hansberry was a child, she and her family lived in a black neighborhood on Chicago's South Side. During this era, segregation—the enforced separation of whites and blacks—was still legal and widespread throughout the South. Northern states, including Hansberry's own Illinois, had no official policy of segregation, but they were generally self-segregated along racial and economic lines. Chicago was a striking example of a city carved into strictly divided black and white neighborhoods. Hansberry's family became one of the first to move into a white neighborhood, but Hansberry still attended a segregated public school for blacks. When neighbors struck at them with threats of violence and legal action, the Hansberrys defended themselves. Hansberry's father successfully brought his case all the way to the Supreme Court.

Hansberry wrote that she always felt the inclination to record her experiences. At times, her writing—including *A Raisin in the Sun*—is recognizably autobiographical. She was one of the first playwrights to create realistic portraits of African-American life. When *A Raisin in the Sun* opened in March 1959, it met with great praise from white and black audience members alike. Arguably the first play to portray black characters, themes, and conflicts in a natural and realistic manner, *A Raisin in the Sun* received the New York Drama Critics' Circle Award for Best Play of the Year. Hansberry was the youngest playwright, the fifth woman, and the only black writer at that point to win the award. She used her new fame to help bring attention to the American civil rights movement as well as African struggles for independence from colonialism. Her promising career was cut short when she died from cancer in 1965, at the age of thirty-four.

A Raisin in the Sun can be considered a turning point in American art because it addresses so many issues important during the 1950s in the United States. The 1950s are widely mocked in modern times as an age of complacency and conformism, symbolized by the growth of suburbs and commercial culture that began in that decade. Such a view, however, is superficial at best. Beneath the eco-nomic prosperity that characterized America in the years following World War II roiled growing domestic and racial tension. The ste-reotype of 1950s America as a land of happy housewives and blacks content with their inferior status resulted in an upswell of social resentment that would finally find public voice in the civil rights and feminist movements of the 1960s. *A Raisin in the Sun,* first performed as the conservative 1950s slid into the radical sixties, explores both of these vital issues.

A Raisin in the Sun was a revolutionary work for its time. Hans-berry creates in the Younger family one of the first honest depictions of a black family on an American stage, in an age when predomi-nantly black audiences simply did not exist. Before this play, Afri-can-American roles, usually small and comedic, largely employed ethnic stereotypes. Hansberry, however, shows an entire black fam-ily in a realistic light, one that is unflattering and far from comedic. She uses black vernacular throughout the play and broaches impor-tant issues and conflicts, such as poverty, discrimination, and the construction of African-American racial identity.

A Raisin in the Sun explores not only the tension between white and black society but also the strain within the black community over how to react to an oppressive white community. Hansberry's drama asks difficult questions about assimilation and identity. Through the character of Joseph Asagai, Hansberry reveals a trend toward celebrating African heritage. As he calls for a native revolt in his homeland, she seems to predict the anticolonial struggles in African countries of the upcoming decades, as well as the inevitabil-ity and necessity of integration.

Hansberry also addressed feminist questions ahead of their time in *A Raisin in the Sun.* Through the character of Beneatha, Hans-berry proposes that marriage is not necessary for women and that women can and should have ambitious career goals. She even ap-proaches an abortion debate, allowing the topic of abortion to enter the action in an era when abortion was illegal. Of course, one of her most radical statements was simply the writing and production of the play—no small feat given her status as a young, black woman in the 1950s.

All of this idealism about race and gender relations boils down to a larger, timeless point—that dreams are crucial. In fact, Hansber-ry's play focuses primarily on the dreams driving and motivating its main characters. These dreams function in positive ways, by lifting their minds from their hard work and tough lifestyle, and in negative ways, by creating in them even more dissatisfaction with their present situations. For the most part, however, the negative dreams come from placing emphasis on materialistic goals rather than on familial pride and happiness. Hansberry seems to argue that as long as people attempt to do their best for their families, they can lift each other up. *A Raisin in the Sun* remains important as a cultural document of a crucial period in American history as well as for the continued debate over racial and gender issues that it has helped spark.

A Note on the Title

Lorraine Hansberry took the title of *A Raisin in the Sun* from a line in Langston Hughes's famous 1951 poem "Harlem: A Dream Deferred." Hughes was a prominent black poet during the 1920s Harlem Renaissance in New York City, during which black artists of all kinds—musicians, poets, writers—gave innovative voices to their personal and cultural experiences. The Harlem Renaissance was a time of immense promise and hopefulness for black artists, as their efforts were noticed and applauded across the United States. In fact, the 1920s are known to history as the Jazz Age, since that musical form, created by a vanguard of black musicians, gained immense national popularity during the period and seemed to embody the exuberance and excitement of the decade. The Harlem Renaissance and the positive national response to the art it produced seemed to herald the possibility of a new age of acceptance for blacks in America.

Langston Hughes was one of the brightest lights of the Harlem Renaissance, and his poems and essays celebrate black culture, creativity, and strength. However, Hughes wrote "Harlem" in 1951, twenty years after the Great Depression crushed the Harlem Renaissance and devastated black communities more terribly than any other group in the United States. In addition, the post–World War II years of the 1950s were characterized by "white flight," in which whites fled the cities in favor of the rapidly growing suburbs. Blacks were often left behind in deteriorating cities, and were unwelcome in the suburbs. In a time of renewed prosperity, blacks were for the most part left behind.

"Harlem" captures the tension between the need for black expression and the impossibility of that expression because of American society's oppression of its black population. In the poem, Hughes asks whether a "dream deferred"—a dream put on hold—withers up "[l]ike a raisin in the sun." His lines confront the racist and dehumanizing attitude prevalent in American society before the civil rights movement of the 1960s that black desires and ambitions were, at best, unimportant and should be ignored, and at worst, should be forcibly resisted. His closing rhetorical question—"*Or does [a dream deferred] explode?*"—is incendiary, a bold statement that the suppression of black dreams might result in an eruption. It implicitly places the blame for this possible eruption on the oppressive society that forces the dream to be deferred. Hansberry's reference to Hughes's poem in her play's title highlights the importance of dreams in *A Raisin in the Sun* and the struggle that her characters face to realize their individual dreams, a struggle inextricably tied to the more fundamental black dream of equality in America.

PLOT OVERVIEW

ARAISIN IN THE SUN portrays a few weeks in the life of the Youngers, an African-American family living on the South Side of Chicago in the 1950s. When the play opens, the Youngers are about to receive an insurance check for $10,000. This money comes from the deceased Mr. Younger's life insurance policy. Each of the adult members of the family has an idea as to what he or she would like to do with this money. The matriarch of the family, Mama, wants to buy a house to fulfill a dream she shared with her husband. Mama's son, Walter Lee, would rather use the money to invest in a liquor store with his friends. He believes that the investment will solve the family's financial problems forever. Walter's wife, Ruth, agrees with Mama, however, and hopes that she and Walter can provide more space and opportunity for their son, Travis. Finally, Beneatha, Walter's sister and Mama's daughter, wants to use the money for her medical school tuition. She also wishes that her family members were not so interested in joining the white world. Beneatha instead tries to find her identity by looking back to the past and to Africa.

As the play progresses, the Youngers clash over their competing dreams. Ruth discovers that she is pregnant but fears that if she has the child, she will put more financial pressure on her family members. When Walter says nothing to Ruth's admission that she is considering abortion, Mama puts a down payment on a house for the whole family. She believes that a bigger, brighter dwelling will help them all. This house is in Clybourne Park, an entirely white neighborhood. When the Youngers' future neighbors find out that the Youngers are moving in, they send Mr. Lindner, from the Clybourne Park Improvement Association, to offer the Youngers money in return for staying away. The Youngers refuse the deal, even after Walter loses the rest of the money ($6,500) to his friend Willy Harris, who persuades Walter to invest in the liquor store and then runs off with his cash.

In the meantime, Beneatha rejects her suitor, George Murchison, whom she believes to be shallow and blind to the problems of race. Subsequently, she receives a marriage proposal from her Nigerian boyfriend, Joseph Asagai, who wants Beneatha to get a medical degree and move to Africa with him (Beneatha does not make her choice before the end of the play). The Youngers eventually move out of the apartment, fulfilling the family's long-held dream. Their future seems uncertain and slightly dangerous, but they are optimistic and determined to live a better life. They believe that they can succeed if they stick together as a family and resolve to defer their dreams no longer.

CHARACTER LIST

Walter Lee Younger The protagonist of the play. Walter is a
dreamer. He wants to be rich and devises plans to
acquire wealth with his friends, particularly Willy
Harris. When the play opens, he wants to invest his
father's insurance money in a new liquor store venture.
He spends the rest of the play endlessly preoccupied
with discovering a quick solution to his family's
various problems.

Beneatha Younger ("Bennie") Mama's daughter and Walter's
sister. Beneatha is an intellectual. Twenty years old,
she attends college and is better educated than the rest
of the Younger family. Some of her personal beliefs
and views have distanced her from conservative
Mama. She dreams of being a doctor and struggles
to determine her identity as a well-educated black
woman.

Lena Younger ("Mama") Walter and Beneatha's mother. The
matriarch of the family, Mama is religious, moral, and
maternal. She wants to use her husband's insurance
money as a down payment on a house with a backyard
to fulfill her dream for her family to move up in the
world.

Ruth Younger Walter's wife and Travis's mother. Ruth takes care
of the Youngers' small apartment. Her marriage to
Walter has problems, but she hopes to rekindle their
love. She is about thirty, but her weariness makes her
seem older. Constantly fighting poverty and domestic
troubles, she continues to be an emotionally strong
woman. Her almost pessimistic pragmatism helps her
to survive.

Travis Younger Walter and Ruth's sheltered young son. Travis earns some money by carrying grocery bags and likes to play outside with other neighborhood children, but he has no bedroom and sleeps on the living-room sofa.

Joseph Asagai A Nigerian student in love with Beneatha. Asagai, as he is often called, is very proud of his African heritage, and Beneatha hopes to learn about her African heritage from him. He eventually proposes marriage to Beneatha and hopes she will return to Nigeria with him.

George Murchison A wealthy, African-American man who courts Beneatha. The Youngers approve of George, but Beneatha dislikes his willingness to submit to white culture and forget his African heritage. He challenges the thoughts and feelings of other black people through his arrogance and flair for intellectual competition.

Mr. Karl Lindner The only white character in the play. Mr. Lindner arrives at the Youngers' apartment from the Clybourne Park Improvement Association. He offers the Youngers a deal to reconsider moving into his (all-white) neighborhood.

Bobo One of Walter's partners in the liquor store plan. Bobo appears to be as mentally slow as his name indicates.

Willy Harris A friend of Walter and coordinator of the liquor store plan. Willy never appears onstage, which helps keep the focus of the story on the dynamics of the Younger family.

Mrs. Johnson The Youngers' neighbor. Mrs. Johnson takes advantage of the Youngers' hospitality and warns them about moving into a predominately white neighborhood.

Analysis of Major Characters

Walter

As Mama's only son, Ruth's defiant husband, Travis's caring father, and Beneatha's belligerent brother, Walter serves as both protagonist and antagonist of the play. The plot revolves around him and the actions that he takes, and his character evolves the most during the course of the play. Most of his actions and mistakes hurt the family greatly, but his belated rise to manhood makes him a sort of hero in the last scene.

Throughout the play, Walter provides an everyman perspective of the mid-twentieth-century African-American male. He is the typical man of the family who struggles to support it and who tries to discover new, better schemes to secure its economic prosperity. Difficulties and barriers that obstruct his and his family's progress to attain that prosperity constantly frustrate Walter. He believes that money will solve all of their problems, but he is rarely successful with money.

Walter often fights and argues with Ruth, Mama, and Beneatha. Far from being a good listener, he does not seem to understand that he must pay attention to his family members' concerns in order to help them. Eventually, he realizes that he cannot raise the family up from poverty alone, and he seeks strength in uniting with his family. Once he begins to listen to Mama and Ruth express their dreams of owning a house, he realizes that buying the house is more important for the family's welfare than getting rich quickly. Walter finally becomes a man when he stands up to Mr. Lindner and refuses the money that Mr. Lindner offers the family not to move in to its dream house in a white neighborhood.

Mama

Mama is Walter and Beneatha's sensitive mother and the head of the Younger household. She demands that members of her family respect themselves and take pride in their dreams. Mama requires that the apartment in which they live always be neat and polished. She stands up for her beliefs and provides perspective from an older generation. She believes in striving to succeed while maintaining her moral boundaries; she rejects Beneatha's progressive and seemingly un-Christian sentiments about God, and Ruth's consideration of an abortion disappoints her. Similarly, when Walter comes to her with his idea to invest in the liquor store venture, she condemns the idea and explains that she will not participate in such un-Christian business. Money is only a means to an end for Mama; dreams are more important to her than material wealth, and her dream is to own a house with a garden and yard in which Travis can play.

Mama is the most nurturing character in the play, and she constantly reminds Walter that all she has ever wanted is to make her children happy and provide for them. She cares deeply for Walter and shows this care by giving him the remaining insurance money. She cares deeply for Ruth as well, consoling her when Walter ignores her. Mama respects Beneatha's assessment of George Murchison as being arrogant and self-centered, telling her daughter not to waste time with such a "fool." Mama loves Travis, her grandchild, and hopes their new house will have a big yard in which he can play. She is also very fond, though in a different way, of her plant, which she tries to nurture throughout the play.

BENEATHA

Beneatha is an attractive college student who provides a young, independent, feminist perspective, and her desire to become a doctor demonstrates her great ambition. Throughout the play, she searches for her identity. She dates two very different men: Joseph Asagai and George Murchison. She is at her happiest with Asagai, her Nigerian boyfriend, who has nicknamed her "Alaiyo," which means "One for Whom Bread—Food—Is Not Enough." She is at her most depressed and angry with George, her pompous, affluent African-American boyfriend. She identifies much more with Asagai's interest in rediscovering his African roots than with George's interest in assimilating into white culture.

Beneatha prides herself on being independent. Asagai criticizes her for being both too independent by not wanting to marry and too dependent by not wanting to leave America. Asagai's wish that Beneatha be quieter and less ambitious obviously outrages her, and his contention late in the play that she has been far from independent—she has had to rely on the insurance money from her father's death and the investments made by her brother to realize her dream of becoming a doctor—greatly influences her. When she realizes this dependence, she gains a new perspective on her dream and a new energy to attain it in her own way. This realization also brings her closer to Walter. While she earlier blames him for his shoddy investing and questions his manhood, she eventually recognizes his strength, a sign that she has become able to appreciate him.

Asagai

One of Beneatha's fellow students and one of her suitors, Asagai is from Nigeria, and throughout the play he provides an international perspective. Proud of his African heritage, he hopes to return to Nigeria to help bring about positive change and modern advancements. He tries to teach Beneatha about her heritage as well. He stands in obvious contrast to Beneatha's other suitor, George Murchison, who is an arrogant African-American who has succeeded in life by assimilating to the white world.

Though Asagai criticizes Beneatha a few times in the play, he seems to do so out of a desire to help her. He criticizes her straightened hair, which resembles Caucasian hair, and persuades her to cut it and keep a more natural, more African look. He criticizes her independent views, but seemingly only to give her new energy and strength. His final criticism of Beneatha—that she is not as independent as she believes herself to be because her dream of attending medical school is bound up in the insurance money from her father's death and her reliance on Walter's investing schemes—further helps to open Beneatha's eyes to the necessity of probing her own existence and identity. The text's implication that Beneatha intends to accept Asagai's proposal of marriage and move to Nigeria with him suggests that he is, in a way, a savior for her.

Themes, Motifs & Symbols

Themes

Themes are the fundamental and often universal ideas explored in a literary work.

The Value and Purpose of Dreams

A Raisin in the Sun is essentially about dreams, as the main characters struggle to deal with the oppressive circumstances that rule their lives. The title of the play references a conjecture that Langston Hughes famously posed in a poem he wrote about dreams that were forgotten or put off. He wonders whether those dreams shrivel up "like a raisin in the sun." Every member of the Younger family has a separate, individual dream—Beneatha wants to become a doctor, for example, and Walter wants to have money so that he can afford things for his family. The Youngers struggle to attain these dreams throughout the play, and much of their happiness and depression is directly related to their attainment of, or failure to attain, these dreams. By the end of the play, they learn that the dream of a house is the most important dream because it unites the family.

The Need to Fight Racial Discrimination

The character of Mr. Lindner makes the theme of racial discrimination prominent in the plot as an issue that the Youngers cannot avoid. The governing body of the Youngers' new neighborhood, the Clybourne Park Improvement Association, sends Mr. Lindner to persuade them not to move into the all-white Clybourne Park neighborhood. Mr. Lindner and the people he represents can only see the color of the Younger family's skin, and his offer to bribe the Youngers to keep them from moving threatens to tear apart the Younger family and the values for which it stands. Ultimately, the Youngers respond to this discrimination with defiance and strength. The play powerfully demonstrates that the way to deal with discrimination is to stand up to it and reassert one's dignity in the face of it rather than allow it to pass unchecked.

THE IMPORTANCE OF FAMILY

The Youngers struggle socially and economically throughout the play but unite in the end to realize their dream of buying a house. Mama strongly believes in the importance of family, and she tries to teach this value to her family as she struggles to keep them together and functioning. Walter and Beneatha learn this lesson about family at the end of the play, when Walter must deal with the loss of the stolen insurance money and Beneatha denies Walter as a brother. Even facing such trauma, they come together to reject Mr. Lindner's racist overtures. They are still strong individuals, but they are now individuals who function as part of a family. When they begin to put the family and the family's wishes before their own, they merge their individual dreams with the family's overarching dream.

MOTIFS

Motifs are recurring structures, contrasts, and literary devices that can help to develop and inform the text's major themes.

THE HOME

The Younger apartment is the only setting throughout the play, emphasizing the centrality of the home. The lighting seems to change with the mood, and with only one window, the apartment is a small, often dark area in which all the Youngers—at one time or another—feel cramped. While some of the play's action occurs outside of the apartment, the audience sees this action play out in the household. Most of what happens outside of the apartment includes Travis's playing out in the street with the rat and Walter's drinking and delinquency from work. The home is a galvanizing force for the family, one that Mama sees as crucial to the family's unity. The audience sees characters outside the family—Joseph Asagai, George Murchison, Mrs. Johnson, Mr. Lindner, and Bobo—only when they visit the apartment. These characters become real through their interactions with the Youngers and the Youngers' reactions to them. The play ends, fittingly, when Mama, lagging behind, finally leaves the apartment.

SYMBOLS

Symbols are objects, characters, figures, and colors used to represent abstract ideas or concepts.

"EAT YOUR EGGS"

This phrase appears early in the play, as an instruction from Ruth to Walter to quiet him. Walter then employs the phrase to illustrate how women keep men from achieving their goals—every time a man gets excited about something, he claims, a woman tries to temper his enthusiasm by telling him to eat his eggs. Being quiet and eating one's eggs represents an acceptance of the adversity that Walter and the rest of the Youngers face in life. Walter believes that Ruth, who is making his eggs, keeps him from achieving his dream, and he argues that she should be more supportive of him. The eggs she makes every day symbolize her mechanical approach to supporting him. She provides him with nourishment, but always in the same, predictable way.

MAMA'S PLANT

The most overt symbol in the play, Mama's plant represents both Mama's care and her dream for her family. In her first appearance onstage, she moves directly toward the plant to take care of it. She confesses that the plant never gets enough light or water, but she takes pride in how it nevertheless flourishes under her care. Her care for her plant is similar to her care for her children, unconditional and unending despite a less-than-perfect environment for growth. The plant also symbolizes her dream to own a house and, more specifically, to have a garden and a yard. With her plant, she practices her gardening skills. Her success with the plant helps her believe that she would be successful as a gardener. Her persistence and dedication to the plant fosters her hope that her dream may come true.

BENEATHA'S HAIR

When the play begins, Beneatha has straightened hair. Midway through the play, after Asagai visits her and questions her hairstyle, she cuts her Caucasian-seeming hair. Her new, radical afro represents her embracing of her heritage. Beneatha's cutting of her hair is a very powerful social statement, as she symbolically declares that natural is beautiful, prefiguring the 1960s cultural credo that black is beautiful. Rather than force her hair to conform to the style society dictates, Beneatha opts for a style that enables her to more easily reconcile her identity and her culture. Beneatha's new hair is a symbol of her anti-assimilationist beliefs as well as her desire to shape her identity by looking back to her roots in Africa.

Summary & Analysis

Act I, scene i

Summary

It is morning at the Youngers' apartment. Their small dwelling on the South Side of Chicago has two bedrooms—one for Mama and Beneatha, and one for Ruth and Walter Lee. Travis sleeps on the couch in the living room. The only window is in their small kitchen, and they share a bathroom in the hall with their neighbors. The stage directions indicate that the furniture, though apparently once chosen with care, is now very worn and faded. Ruth gets up first and after some noticeable difficulty, rouses Travis and Walter as she makes breakfast. While Travis gets ready in the communal bathroom, Ruth and Walter talk in the kitchen. They do not seem happy, yet they engage in some light humor. They keep mentioning a check. Walter scans the front page of the newspaper and reads that another bomb was set off, and Ruth responds with indifference. Travis asks them for money—he is supposed to bring fifty cents to school—and Ruth says that they do not have it. His persistent nagging quickly irritates her. Walter, however, gives Travis an entire dollar while staring at Ruth. Travis then leaves for school, and Walter tells Ruth that he wants to use the check to invest in a liquor store with a few of his friends. Walter and Ruth continue to argue about their unhappy lives, a dialogue that Ruth cuts short by telling her husband, "Eat your eggs, they gonna be cold."

Beneatha gets up next and after discovering that the bathroom is occupied by someone from another family, engages in a verbal joust with Walter. He thinks that she should be doing something more womanly than studying medicine, especially since her tuition will cut into the check, which is the insurance payment for their father's death. Beneatha argues that the money belongs to Mama and that Mama has the right to decide how it is spent. Walter then leaves for his job as a chauffeur—he has to ask Ruth for money to get to work because the money he gave Travis was his car fare. Mama enters and goes directly to a small plant that she keeps just outside the kitchen window. She expresses sympathy for her grandson, Travis, while she questions Ruth's ability to care for him properly. She asks Ruth what she would do with the money, which amounts to $10,000. For once, Ruth seems to be on Walter's side. She thinks that if Mama gives him some of the money he might regain his happiness and confidence, which are two things Ruth feels she can no longer provide for Walter. Mama, though, feels morally repulsed by the idea of getting into the liquor business. Instead, she wants to move to a house with a lawn on which Travis can play. Owning a house had always been a dream she had shared with her husband, and now that he is gone she nurtures this dream even more powerfully.

Mama and Ruth begin to tease Beneatha about the many activities that she tries and quits, including her latest attempt to learn how to play the guitar. Beneatha claims that she is trying to "express" herself, an idea at which Ruth and Mama have a laugh. They discuss the man that Beneatha has been dating, George Murchison. Beneatha gets angry as they praise George because she thinks that he is "shallow." Mama and Ruth do not understand her ambivalence toward George, arguing that she should like him simply because he is rich. Beneatha contends that, for that very reason, any further relationship is pointless, as George's family wouldn't approve of her anyway. Beneatha makes the mistake of using the Lord's name in vain in front of Mama, which sparks another conversation about the extent of God's providence. Beneatha argues that God does not seem to help her or the family. Mama, outraged at such a pronouncement, asserts that she is head of the household and that there will be no such thoughts expressed in her home. Beneatha recants and leaves for school, and Mama goes to the window to tend her plant. Ruth and Mama talk about Walter and Beneatha, and Ruth suddenly faints.

ANALYSIS

All of the characters in *A Raisin in the Sun* have unfulfilled dreams. These dreams mostly involve money. Although the Younger family seems alienated from white middle-class culture, they harbor the same materialistic dreams as the rest of American society. In the 1950s, the stereotypical American dream was to have a house with a yard, a big car, and a happy family. The Youngers also seem to want to live this dream, though their struggle to attain any semblance of it is dramatically different from the struggle a similar suburban family might encounter, because the Youngers are not a stereotypical middle-class family. Rather, they live in a world in which being middle class is also a dream.

Mama's plant symbolizes her version of this dream, because she cares for it as she cares for her family. She tries to give the plant enough light and water not only to grow but also to flourish and become beautiful, just as she attempts to provide for her family with meager yet consistent financial support. Mama also imagines a garden that she can tend along with her dream house. The small potted plant acts as a temporary stand-in for her much larger dream. Her relentless care for the plant represents her protection of her dream. Despite her cramped living situation and the lifetime of hard work that she has endured, she maintains her focus on her dream, which helps her to persevere. Still, no matter how much Mama works, the plant remains feeble, because there is so little light. Similarly, it is difficult for her to care for her family as much as she wants and to have her family members grow as much as she wants. Her dream of a house and a better life for her family remains tenuous because it is so hard for her to see beyond her family's present situation.

Beneatha's dream differs from Mama's in that it is, in many ways, self-serving. In her desires to "express" herself and to become a doctor, Beneatha proves an early feminist who radically views her role as self-oriented and not family-oriented. Feminism had not fully emerged into the American cultural landscape when Hansberry wrote *A Raisin in the Sun,* and Beneatha seems a prototype for the more enthusiastic feminism of the 1960s and 1970s. She not only wants to have a career—a far cry from the June Cleaver stay-at-home-mom role models of the 1950s (June Cleaver was the name of the mother on *Leave it to Beaver,* a popular late-1950s sitcom about a stereotypical suburban family)—but also desires to find her identity and pursue an independent career without relying solely on a man. She even indicates to Ruth and Mama that she might not get married, a possibility that astonishes them because it runs counter to their expectations of a woman's role. Similarly, they are befuddled by her dislike of the "pretty, rich" George Murchison. That Beneatha's attitude toward him differs from Ruth's or Mama's may result from the age difference among the three women. Mama and Beneatha are, of course, a generation apart, while Ruth occupies a place somewhere in the middle; Hansberry argues that Beneatha is the least traditional of the women because she is the youngest.

Walter and Ruth, who occupy the middle ground in terms of age between Mama and Beneatha, have also tempered their dreams more than Beneatha has. Though Walter and Ruth harbor materialistic dreams, they desire wealth not solely for self-serving purposes but rather as a means to provide for their family and escape the South Side ghetto in which they live. The tension evoked by issues of money and manhood comes sharply into focus when Travis asks for fifty cents. Ruth, the household manager, refuses to give her son the money; Walter, as a father trying to safeguard his son's ability to be accepted, gives Travis twice as much as he asks for. Walter does so knowing that he faces the emasculating task of having to ask Ruth for money himself as a result. As the two talk about their entrapping situation, Ruth's reply of "[e]at your eggs" answers every statement that Walter offers, reflecting the stereotypical perception that blacks have an inability to overcome problems.

ACT I, SCENE II

> *Once upon a time freedom used to be life—now it's money.*
>
> *(See* QUOTATIONS, *p. 35)*

SUMMARY

The next day, Saturday, the Youngers are cleaning their apartment and waiting for the insurance check to arrive. Walter receives a phone call from his friend Willy Harris, who is coordinating the potential liquor store venture. It appears that their plan is moving smoothly. The insurance check is all Walter needs to pursue the venture. He promises to bring the money to Willy when he receives it. Meanwhile, Beneatha is spraying the apartment with insecticide in an attempt to rid it of cockroaches. Beneatha and Travis start fighting, and Beneatha threatens him with the spray gun.

The phone rings, and Beneatha answers. She invites the person on the phone over to the still-dirty apartment, much to Mama's chagrin. After hanging up, Beneatha explains to Mama that the man she has spoken to on the phone is Joseph Asagai, an African intellectual whom Beneatha has met at school. She and Mama discuss Beneatha's worries about her family's ignorance about Africa and African people. Mama believes that Africans need religious salvation from "heathenism," while Beneatha believes that they are in greater need of political and civil salvation from French and British colonialism.

Ruth returns from seeing a doctor, who has told her that she is two months pregnant. She reveals this information to Mama and Beneatha. Ruth and Beneatha are worried and uncertain, while

Mama simply expresses her hope that the baby will be a girl. Ruth calls the doctor "she," which arouses Mama's suspicion because their family doctor is a man. Ruth feels ill and anxious about her pregnancy. Mama tries to help her relax.

Asagai visits Beneatha, and they spend some time together by themselves. He brings her some Nigerian clothing and music as gifts. As Beneatha tries on one of the robes, Asagai asks about her straightened hair. He implies that her hairstyle is too American and unnatural, and he wonders how it got that way. Beneatha says that her hair was once like his, but that she finds it too "raw" that way. He teases her a bit about being very serious about finding her identity, particularly her African identity, through him. Asagai obviously cares for Beneatha very much, and he wonders why Beneatha does not have the same feeling for him. She explains that she is looking for more than storybook love. She wants to become an independent and liberated woman. Asagai scorns her wish, much to Beneatha's disappointment.

Mama comes into the room, and Beneatha introduces her to Asagai. Mama then recites Beneatha's views on Africa and African people as best she can. When Asagai says goodbye, he calls Beneatha by a nickname, "Alaiyo." He explains that it is a word from his African tribal language, roughly translated to mean "One for Whom Bread—Food—Is Not Enough." He leaves, having charmed both women. Finally, the check arrives.

Walter returns home and wants to talk about his liquor store plans. Ruth wants to discuss her pregnancy with him and becomes upset when he will not listen. She shuts herself into their bedroom. Mama sits down with Walter who is upset by—and ashamed of—his poverty, his job as a chauffeur, and his lack of upward mobility. Finally, Mama tells him that Ruth is pregnant and that she fears that Ruth is considering having an abortion. Walter does not believe that Ruth would do such a thing until Ruth comes out of the bedroom to confirm that she has made a down payment on the service.

ANALYSIS

While the play takes place entirely within the Youngers' apartment, Hansberry takes care to introduce external influences. This scene includes two phone calls: one for Walter from Willy about the liquor store investment and the other for Beneatha from Joseph Asagai, her good friend and fellow intellectual. These phone calls serve parallel functions for those who receive them and demonstrate what is important to both of the characters: Walter is waiting to move quickly on the investment, while Beneatha cannot wait to see Asagai and introduce him to her family.

Beneatha's spraying of the apartment seems symbolic of her dissatisfaction with her surroundings. She wants to rid herself and her family of what she later refers to as "acute ghetto-itis." It is obvious that Beneatha is not proud of her family's economic and social situation and is a bit embarrassed by it when Asagai visits. As she asks him to sit down, she scurries to throw the spray gun off the couch in the hopes that Asagai won't see it. Interestingly, Beneatha's spraying reverses the pattern the Youngers' dreams. While most of their dreams involve the acquisition of some markers of success, such as a home, large cars, and privileged education, Beneatha has to begin by first ridding herself of the bugs that plague her current situation.

The interaction between Beneatha and Asagai reveals how serious Beneatha is about finding her identity. Beneatha does not want to assimilate into, or become successful in, the dominant white culture of the 1950s. Yet while she wants to break free of conforming to the white ideal, she still wants to acclimate herself to an educated American life. Many African-American intellectuals and writers, especially in the 1960s, faced this dilemma; Beneatha's character thus seems somewhat ahead of her time. Indeed, her seeking of her roots in Africa to forge her identity (even though her family has been in America for five generations) precedes the New African movement of the 1960s. In this movement, African-Americans embraced their racial history, stopping their attempts to assimilate, even in physical appearance. Asagai hints at what is to come by telling Beneatha that by straightening her hair she is "mutilating" it. In his opinion, her hair should look as it does naturally: she should stop straightening it to look like white hair and instead wear an afro. Unsure of her identity as an African-American woman joining an overwhelmingly white world, Beneatha turns to Asagai to see if he can supply a lost part of her self.

This scene also reveals Walter's growing restlessness, as well as the desperation with which Ruth is trying to hold her family together. Ruth does not want to have an abortion, but she considers it because she sees it as the only way to keep the family together. It is possible that Hansberry is attempting to make a bold feminist statement with this plot twist. During the 1950s, abortion was illegal, but Ruth has valid reasons for not wanting her pregnancy. Obviously,

Ruth is not an immoral or evil woman. She simply wants to do the best for the family that she already has. Walter, on the other hand, lacks this singular dedication to his family. His character is meant to represent a kind of broken masculinity that society perceived among African-American men of the 1950s, men who were shut out of the American dream by racism and poverty. Because of this exclusion, Walter's dreams of money and success in business become inextricably linked to his image of himself as a man.

Through the announcement of Ruth's pregnancy, we can see the power that Mama wields as the matriarch of the family. She is at the center of her family's life, and she controls many of the interactions of the members of her household. Actresses seem to portray the character of Mama in two primary ways: either as a folksy relic of an earlier time, a woman who hopes one day to have a garden in the sun, or more recently, as a hardworking, powerful, all-knowing matriarch. Both interpretations seem valid. She reminds the family of the importance of family and history, and she holds the power to make economic decisions. She does so literally in this scene by holding the insurance check.

Act II, scene i

Summary

Later on the same Saturday, Beneatha emerges from her room cloaked in the Nigerian clothes that Asagai has brought her. She dances around the apartment, claiming to be performing a tribal dance while shouting "OCOMOGOSIAY" and singing. Ruth finds Beneatha's pageantry silly and questions her about it. Meanwhile, Walter returns home drunk. He sees Beneatha all dressed up and acts out some made-up tribal rituals with her, at one point standing on a table and pronouncing himself "Flaming Spear." Ruth looks on wearily.

George Murchison arrives to pick up Beneatha. Beneatha removes her headdress to reveal that she has cut off most of her hair, leaving only an unstraightened afro. Everyone is shocked, amazed, and slightly disappointed with Beneatha, prompting a fierce discussion between Beneatha and George about the importance of their African heritage. Beneatha goes to change for the theater, and Walter talks to George about business plans. George does not seem interested. Walter then becomes belligerent as he makes fun of George's white shoes. Embarrassed, Ruth explains that the white shoes are part of the "college *style*." George obviously looks down on Walter—calling him "Prometheus"—and Walter gets even angrier at him. George and Beneatha finally leave, and Ruth and Walter then begin to fight about Walter going out, spending money, and interacting with people like Willy Harris. They do begin to make up, though, by acknowledging that a great distance has grown between them.

Mama comes home and announces that she has put a down payment on a house with some of the insurance money. Ruth is elated to hear this news because she too dreams of moving out of their current apartment and into a more respectable home. Meanwhile, Walter is noticeably upset because he wants to put all the money into the liquor store venture. They all become worried when they hear that the house is in Clybourne Park, an entirely white neighborhood. Mama asks for their understanding—it was the only house that they could afford. She feels she needs to buy the house to hold the family together. Ruth regains her pleasure and rejoices, but Walter feels betrayed, his dream swept under the table. Walter makes Mama feel guilty, saying that she has crushed his dream. He goes quickly to his bedroom, and Mama remains sitting and worrying.

ANALYSIS

Beneatha's exploration of her African heritage and her entrance with her afro and Nigerian garb were perhaps the first such appearance on an American stage. Hansberry creates a radical character in Beneatha, one who does not willingly submit to what she calls "oppressive" white culture. Since the audience for this play's initial run was mostly white, such a threat to white dominance was extremely revolutionary.

The dancing scene with Beneatha and Walter is difficult to interpret, as the drunken Walter seems to mock the African dances and practices, while Beneatha seems not to comprehend this mocking. In addition, Beneatha's fight with George and the rest of her family represents a larger battle within the black community over whether to enhance and celebrate their differences from whites or whether to join white culture and try to elevate their status within it. This desire to join white culture, referred to as assimilationism, was a contentious issue for the black community in the 1950s and 1960s. The overall tone of this scene seems to be anti-assimilationist—that is, the scene seems to value Beneatha's expression of her cultural roots.

Beneatha's two suitors embody this dichotomy between the conflicting identities available to blacks: the identity that seeks assimilation and the identity that rejects assimilation. This scene separates George and Asagai into completely different categories where George, as his common name suggests, represents a black person assimilating into the white world, while Asagai, with his ethnically rich name, stands for the New Africanist culture that those who oppose assimilation pursue. As Beneatha dances in a robe that Asagai gives her, George deems her interest in her African roots absurd. His comments put him further at odds with Beneatha, and she begins to feel more of an affinity with Asagai and her African roots than with George and what she considers to be his false roots in American society.

Ruth and Walter's conversation reveals that they do have love left in their marriage and that they have both been oppressed by their circumstances. Their entrapment in the ghetto, in their jobs, and in their apartment results in the desire to leave physically, to escape mentally through alcohol, and to lash out at those involved in the entrapment. One way for them to escape this entrapment, though, seems to be through a reliance on each other. Yet, often, circumstances are so difficult for them that they cannot even do that. They continue to fight, as they put their own concerns before each other's and before their marriage.

Mama's down payment on a house reveals her belief that to be a happy family the Youngers need to own space and property. Her dream is a perfect example of the quintessential American dream. Part of her dream is the simple desire for consumer goods. She believes, as did many in the post–World War II consumer culture, that, to some degree at least, ownership can provide happiness. Therefore, although she means only to find the best for her family, she also succumbs to the powerful materialism that drives the desires of the society around her. Still, her desire is somewhat radical, because African-Americans were largely left out of depictions of the American dream during this period. Only white families populated suburban television programs and magazine advertisements. Therefore, Hansberry performs a radical act in claiming the general American dream for African-Americans.

The radical nature of the Youngers' desire to participate in the American dream does bring along some hardship. Ruth and Walter's concern about moving into a predominantly white neighborhood reflects the great tension that existed between races—even in the

Northern states. Their concern foreshadows, among other develop-
ments, the arrival of Mr. Lindner, who reveals that the white people
of Clybourne Park are just as wary of the Youngers as the Youngers
are of white people.

ACT II, SCENE II

> *[Y]our daddy's gonna make a . . . business transaction
> that's going to change our lives. . . . You just name it,
> son . . . and I hand you the world!*
>
> *(See* QUOTATIONS, *p. 37)*

SUMMARY

On a Friday night a few weeks later, Beneatha and George return
from a date. The Youngers' apartment is full of moving boxes.
George wants to kiss Beneatha, but she does not want to kiss.
Rather, she wants to engage George in a conversation about the
plight of African-Americans. It seems that George wants to marry a
"nice . . . simple . . . sophisticated girl." Mama comes in as Beneatha
kicks him out. Mama asks if she had a good time with George, and
Beneatha tells her that George is a "fool." Mama replies, "I guess
you better not waste your time with no fools." Beneatha appreciates
her mother's support.

Mrs. Johnson—the Youngers' neighbor—visits. Mama and Ruth
offer her food and drink, and she gladly accepts. She has come to
visit to tell them about a black family who has been bombed out of
their home in a white neighborhood. She is generally insensitive and
unable to speak in a civil manner. She predicts that the Youngers will
also be scared out of the all-white neighborhood once they move
in and insults much of the family by calling them a "proud-acting
bunch of colored folks." She then quotes Booker T. Washington, a
famous African-American thinker and assimilationist. A frustrated
and angered Mama retaliates by calling him a "fool." Mrs. Johnson
leaves the apartment.

Walter's boss calls, telling Ruth that Walter has not been to work
in three days. Walter explains that he has been wandering all day
(often way into the country) and drinking all night (at a bar with
a jazz duo that he loves). He says that he feels depressed, despon-
dent, and useless as the man of the family. He feels that his job is
no better than a slave's job. Mama feels guilty for his unhappiness
and tells him that she has never done anything to hurt her children.

She gives him the remaining $6,500 of the insurance money, telling him to deposit $3,000 for Beneatha's education and to keep the last $3,500. With this money, Mama says, Walter should become—and should act like he has become—the head of the family. Walter suddenly becomes more confident and energized. He talks to Travis about his plans, saying that he is going to "make a transaction" that will make them rich. Walter's excitement builds as he describes his dream of their future house and cars, as well as Travis's potential college education.

ANALYSIS

In Beneatha and George's conversation, Hansberry reveals two sets of values regarding education. Beneatha believes in education as a means to understanding and self-fulfillment, while George sees education as a means to get a good job. The difference in their views about education displays a deeper divergence between the two, one of idealism versus pragmatism. Beneatha believes that society must be changed through self-knowledge and, thus, through consciousness and celebration of one's heritage. George and his family, however, believe that they should become wealthy and perhaps achieve respect through their economic status, which demands a certain degree of assimilation into the dominant, white culture. Though George's wealth and bearing impress Mama at first, she eventually shares Beneatha's point of view.

Indeed, in the episode with Mrs. Johnson, it becomes clear that Mama agrees with Beneatha far more than one might expect. This scene portrays both George Murchison and Booker T. Washington as assimilationists, and Mama refers to them both as "fools." While Mama calls George a "fool" only in response to Beneatha's remark, her branding of Booker T. Washington with such an insult has profound historical and cultural implications. Washington, historically a hero to many in the black community, preached assimilation into mainstream America as the primary goal of African-Americans. Though he attained great stature in the first half of the twentieth century, public opinion had turned against him by the late 1950s. Many African-Americans had begun to reject assimilationist ideals, believing by this time that mainstream America would always mean white America and that assimilating into this culture would always mean degrading themselves to fit white society's perceptions of how blacks should be and act. These African-Americans thus sought an independent identity that would allow them to embrace and express their heritage and culture.

The scene closes with Walter's description to Travis of his materialistic fantasy about the future—Walter still wants to be a part of the culture that excludes him. He wants to be rich if being rich is the solution to his family's problems. Most of all, he wants his son to have a better life than he has had and wants to provide him with the education he deserves. His wish for Travis seems selfish as well; he wants desperately to feel like a man, and he believes that Travis's success would reflect on his own success as the man of the house.

Walter's view of education seems to fall somewhere between Beneatha's and George's views. Walter seems to care more for Travis's education than for Beneatha's, partly because Travis is his child and partly because Beneatha is a woman. Within the marginalized group of blacks exists the even more marginalized group of black women who have to fight with prejudice across both racial and gender lines. Walter, whether consciously or not, is acting as if his and his son's interests are more important than Beneatha's, even though Beneatha has proven she is intellectually capable. Walter believes that the insurance money Mama gives him can provide him with financial success and educational resources for his son, a priority he values more highly than his sister's goal of becoming a doctor.

Act II, scene iii

Summary

On Saturday, a week later, it is moving day. Ruth shows Beneatha the curtains she has bought for the new house and tells her that the first thing she is going to do in their new house is take a long bath in their very own bathroom. Ruth comments on the changed mood around the household, noting that she and Walter even went out to the movies and held hands the previous evening. Walter comes in and dances with Ruth. Beneatha teases them about acting in a stereotypical fashion but does not really mean any harm. Ruth and Walter understand and join in the lighthearted teasing, and Walter claims that Beneatha talks about nothing but race.

A middle-aged white man named Karl Lindner appears at the door. He is a representative from the Clybourne Park Improvement Association, and he tells the Youngers that problems arise when different kinds of people do not sit down and talk to each other. The Youngers agree, until he reveals that he and the neighborhood coalition believe that the Youngers' presence in Clybourne Park would destroy the community there. The current residents are all white, working-class people who do not want anything to threaten the dream that they have for their community. Mr. Lindner tells the Youngers that the association is prepared to offer them more money than they are to pay for the house in exchange for not moving to Clybourne Park. Ruth, Beneatha, and Walter all become very upset, but they manage to control their anger. Walter firmly tells Mr. Lindner that they will not accept the offer and urges Mr. Lindner to leave immediately.

When Mama comes home, Walter, Ruth, and Beneatha tell her about Mr. Lindner's visit. It shocks and worries her, but she supports their decision to refuse the buyout offer. Then, as she is making sure that her plant is well packed for the trip, the rest of the family surprises her with gifts of gardening tools and a huge gardening hat. Mama has never received presents other than at Christmas, and she is touched by her family's generosity. Just as the whole family begins to celebrate, Bobo, one of Walter's friends, arrives. After some stumbling, he announces that Willy Harris has run off with all of the money that Walter invested in the liquor store deal. It turns out that Walter had invested not only his $3,500 but also the $3,000 intended for Beneatha's education. Mama is livid and begins to beat Walter in the face. Beneatha breaks them up. Weakness overcomes Mama, and she thinks about the hard labor her husband endured in order to earn the money for them. She prays ardently for strength.

ANALYSIS

This scene presents two conflicts and worries for the Youngers and their future. First, the incident with Mr. Lindner of the Clybourne Park Improvement Association reveals the power of both dreams and racial prejudice. Mr. Lindner's comments do not intimidate the members of the Younger family. Rather, they seem to expect the conflict. The Youngers know that they are about to achieve some of their dreams and are not going to let racism get in their way. Mama's careful packing of her plant when she hears of the incident shows she is proud of her fortitude in holding onto her dream. She knows that she needs a token of the dream's power in order to face hardship in the all-white neighborhood. The plant symbolizes her dream of escaping from their poverty-stricken life. It also represents a dream for African-American equality and acceptance in the general culture. In addition, this episode shows that the fact that Mama holds onto her dream is as important as the realization of this dream.

The second conflict, Walter's duplicitous investment of the insurance money and its disastrous result, evokes much greater strife and discord. When Bobo arrives and announces that the money is gone, Walter yells, "THAT MONEY IS MADE OUT OF MY FATHER'S FLESH," reflecting his belief that money is the lifeblood of human existence. None of the Youngers feels pity for Walter, and it seems now that none of their dreams will come true. Ruth and Beneatha reach a new low of depression and pessimism. While Mama protests at first, she seems to agree with their attitude when she talks about watching her husband wither from hard work. In the face of the loss of the money, Mama's idealism about family falters. Mama's sudden sad realization that her husband's life boils down to a stack of paper bills compels her to turn on Walter as if he had killed his father himself. This anger is uncommon for Mama, and it is significant because it demonstrates that her compassion is not born of passivity. She cares too much for the memory of her husband, for their mutual dream of buying a home, and for her family to let Walter off the hook. Her beating him is the only way for her to force Walter to realize his mistakes and to look for a way to correct them.

Though the other characters talk about Willy Harris, the man who runs away with Walter's and Bobo's money, he never makes an appearance onstage. Willy remains a faceless symbol for Walter's negligence and risky handling of the money. Moreover, Hansberry's focus is not on the act of theft but rather on the Younger family and the reactions of its members to adversity.

ACT III

SUMMARY

*I will go home and much of what I will have to say
will seem strange to the people of my village. But I will
teach and work and things will happen, slowly and
swiftly.*

(*See* QUOTATIONS, *p. 39*)

One hour later on moving day, everyone is still melancholy. The
stage directions indicate that even the light in the apartment looks
gray. Walter sits alone and thinks. Asagai comes to help them pack
and finds Beneatha questioning her choice of becoming a doctor. She
no longer believes that she can help people. Instead of feeling ideal-
istic about demanding equality for African-Americans and freeing
Africans from the French and English colonizers, she now broods
about basic human misery. Never-ending human misery demoral-
izes her, and she no longer sees a reason to fight against it. Asagai
reprimands her for her lack of idealism and her attachment to the
money from her father's death. He tells Beneatha about his dream to
return to Africa and help bring positive changes. He gets her excited
about reform again and asks her to go home with him to Africa,
saying that eventually it would be as if she had "only been away for
a day." He leaves her alone to think about his proposition.

Walter rushes in from the bedroom and out the door amid a sar-
castic monologue from Beneatha. Mama enters and announces that
they are not going to move. Ruth protests. Walter returns, having
called Mr. Lindner and invited him back to the apartment—he intends to take his offer of money in exchange for not moving to Clybourne Park. Everyone objects to this plan, arguing that they have
too much pride to accept not being able to live somewhere because
of their race. Walter, very agitated, puts on an act, imitating the
stereotype of a black male servant. When he finally exits, Mama declares that he has died inside. Beneatha decides that he is no longer
her brother, but Mama reminds her to love him, especially when he
is so downtrodden.

The movers and Mr. Lindner arrive. Mama tells Walter to deal
with Mr. Lindner, who is laying out contracts for Walter to sign.
Walter starts hesitantly, but soon we see that he has changed his
mind about taking Mr. Lindner's money. His speech builds in power.
He tells Mr. Lindner that the Youngers are proud and hardworking

and intend to move into their new house. Mr. Lindner appeals to Mama, who defers to Walter's statement. Ultimately, Mr. Lindner leaves with his papers unsigned. Everyone finishes packing up as the movers come to take the furniture. Mama tells Ruth that she thinks Walter has finally become a man by standing up to Mr. Lindner. Ruth agrees and is noticeably proud of her husband. Mama, who is the last to leave, looks for a moment at the empty apartment. Then she leaves, bringing her plant with her.

> *There is always something left to love. And if you ain't learned that, you ain't learned nothing.*
>
> (See QUOTATIONS, *p. 40*)

> *[W]e have decided to move into our house. . . . We don't want to make no trouble for nobody or fight no causes, and we will try to be good neighbors.*
>
> (See QUOTATIONS, *p. 41*)

ANALYSIS

Though this act begins in despair, the Youngers regain hope and motivation to pursue their dreams as it continues. Asagai renews Beneatha's courage and pride. His discussion of colonial Africa and his stated belief that the ruling powers must fall predicts the unrest that was to occur in those countries in the decades following the 1950s. Asagai's claim that when Beneatha arrives in Africa she will feel as if she has been gone for only a day is a claim that America can never be home to blacks, no matter how long they have lived there.

Asagai's radicalism, which Hansberry seems to endorse, is somewhat problematic. As an extreme position of anti-assimilationism, Asagai's views differ little from self-segregation. In practical terms, Asagai's desire to leave white America and Mr. Lindner's desire to keep African-Americans out of his neighborhood have a similar basis—the rejection of integration. Each man wants to preserve his notion of cultural identity, one through returning to an African homeland and the other through racist extortion tactics. After all, as a Nigerian, Asagai has a distinct cultural identity to preserve, and arguably, Mr. Lindner has one as well. But Beneatha, as a black American, does not have a clear-cut cultural identity. Her ancestry may originate in Africa, but she has never been there. She and her immediate relatives have all grown up in Chicago. Though racial lines definitely exist between the area in which the Youngers currently live and the area to which they plan to move, the working-class neighborhood of Clybourne Park is clearly not an entire world away from the South Side. In harmony with an age-old argument about racial identity, it seems that the color lines that engender wrongful prejudice on the part of some (white society at large) are being reinforced by a movement (black anti-assimilationism) to establish a minority characterized by those lines. Beneatha, after all, understands the working-class plight and language of the white people of Clybourne Park, while she is, at least initially, wholly ignorant of the language and customs of West Africa.

While Hansberry seems to use Asagai and Beneatha to make a radical point about race, she also returns Beneatha to a conservative position in terms of her feminism. Whereas Beneatha claims at the beginning of the play that she might not marry, Asagai's marriage proposal sweeps her off of her feet. According to the stage directions, she mentions it to her mother, "[g]irlishly and unreasonably trying to pursue the conversation." From a feminist perspective, Hansberry seems to abandon Beneatha's development. The status of Beneatha's education remains ambiguous, but it is clear that she intends to accept Asagai's proposal, his beliefs, and his dreams. She maintains her independence from female convention by accepting Asagai and rejecting the financially secure and socially acceptable George Murchison. Other aspects of her previously expressed self-reliance and strong beliefs in education remain unresolved.

Walter's dream for money and material goods remains unrealized, but he has modified his dream as he has matured. While he almost succumbs to accepting Mr. Lindner's money, his family convinces him that they have worked too hard to have anyone tell them where they can and cannot live. In other words, his pride, work, and humanity become more important to him than his dream of money. Walter finally "come[s] into his manhood," as Mama says, recognizing that being proud of his family is more important than having money. For Walter, the events of the play are a rite of passage. He must endure challenges in order to arrive at a more adult understanding of the important things in life.

While both of her children achieve happiness but incomplete fulfillment of their dreams, Mama realizes her dream of moving at last. As the matriarch and oldest member of the family, Mama is a testament to the potential of dreams, since she has lived to see the dream she and her husband shared fulfilled. The younger Youngers, aptly named to show the shifting emphasis from old to young, are at midpoints in their lives. With the new house, they are well on their way to the complete fulfillment of their dreams. Mama's last moment in the apartment and her transporting of her plant show that although she is happy about moving, she continues to cherish the memories she has accumulated throughout her life. Hansberry implies, then, that the sweetness of dream fulfillment accompanies the sweetness of the dream itself. Mama pauses on her way out of the apartment to show respect and appreciation for the hard work that went into making the dream come true. Her husband lingers in her recollections, and when she says to Ruth a few lines earlier, "Yeah—they something all right, my children," it becomes almost an invocation of their unmistakably solid futures.

Important Quotations Explained

1. MAMA: Oh—So now it's life. Money is life. Once upon a time freedom used to be life—now it's money. I guess the world really do change . . .

   WALTER: No—it was always money, Mama. We just didn't know about it.

   MAMA: No . . . something has changed. You something new, boy. In my time we was worried about not being lynched . . . You ain't satisfied or proud of nothing we done. I mean that you had a home; that we kept you out of trouble till you was grown; that you don't have to ride to work on the back of nobody's streetcar—You my children—but how different we done become.

This exchange occurs in Act I, scene ii when Mama asks Walter why he always talks about money. Walter responds that "[m]oney is life," explaining to her that success is now defined by how much money one has. This conversation takes place early in the play and reveals Mama's and Walter's economic struggles. These lines demonstrate the ideological differences between their generations. Throughout the play, Mama's views are at odds with Walter's and Beneatha's views. For Walter, money seems to be the answer to everything. Money, he believes, allows people to live comfortable and carefree lives. It also seems to define a man by measuring his success and ability to provide for his family. For Walter, who feels enslaved in his job and life, money is the truest freedom.

Throughout *A Raisin in the Sun*, characters connect money to discussions of race. Mama says, "Once upon a time freedom used to be life—now it's money. I guess the world really do change." Walter grew up being "free" in the way that Mama means, but he faced other problems, such as the lack of financial and social freedom that he talks about here. Walter believes that freedom is not enough

35

and that, while civil rights are a large step for blacks, in the real world—for the Youngers, the South Side of Chicago in the 1940s and 1950s—blacks are still treated differently and more harshly than whites. Mr. Lindner, who later comes to persuade the Youngers not to move into his all-white neighborhood, embodies one example of this racist treatment. Mrs. Johnson later speaks of reading about the bombing of a black family's house in the "colored paper" and complains that the racist white people who were responsible for the bombing make her feel like times have not changed, as if they still live in turbulent Mississippi, a hotbed of racism during the mid-twentieth century.

QUOTATIONS

2. WALTER: You wouldn't understand yet, son, but your daddy's gonna make a transaction . . . a business transaction that's going to change our lives. . . . That's how come one day when you 'bout seventeen years old I'll come home . . . I'll pull the car up on the driveway . . . just a plain black Chrysler, I think, with white walls— no—black tires . . . the gardener will be clipping away at the hedges and he'll say, "Good evening, Mr. Younger." And I'll say, "Hello, Jefferson, how are you this evening?" And I'll go inside and Ruth will come downstairs and meet me at the door and we'll kiss each other and she'll take my arm and we'll go up to your room to see you sitting on the floor with the catalogues of all the great schools in America around you. . . . All the great schools in the world! And—and I'll say, all right son—it's your seventeenth birthday, what is it you've decided? . . . Just tell me, what it is you want to be—and you'll be it. . . . Whatever you want to be—Yessir! You just name it, son . . . and I hand you the world!

This speech from Act II, scene ii, which Walter delivers to Travis as he tucks him in bed, closes an important scene and foreshadows the climax of the play. Walter explains to Travis, and to the audience, that he will move quickly to invest the money that Mama has just given him (part of it meant for Beneatha's future schooling costs).

Walter seems to be rehashing conversations he might have heard while he was working as a chauffer to rich people. That he envisions having a gardener makes it seem that Walter wants to live a life that he has seen others enjoy and be like the people he has serviced. He explains his dream of the future in detail, as if it were being presented before his eyes. He paints the future vividly, even describing what sort of tires his cars will have and how busy his day will be with important matters. He never speaks in the conditional mood, which entails words such as "if" and "would" and suggests uncertainty, but in the future tense, using the word "will" throughout. This use of the future tense makes his dream appear to be something that will inevitably come true.

Yet Walter's dream is not entirely materialistic. He envisions a better relationship with his wife, Ruth, in which they kiss and hold hands—a far cry from the relationship they have now. He also explains to Travis that he will have his choice among all the best colleges and that they will have enough money to send him to whichever one he chooses. At heart, Walter wants to provide for his family and reduce their cares.

3. ASAGAI: Then isn't there something wrong in a house—in a world—where all dreams, good or bad, must depend on the death of a man?

BENEATHA: AND YOU CANNOT ANSWER IT!

ASAGAI: I LIVE THE ANSWER!

This exchange occurs near the end of the play in Act III, as Asagai and Beneatha fight after Bobo comes to tell the Youngers that the money Walter has invested is gone. Beneatha is terribly depressed and cynical, knowing now that the money for her future education is also gone and that her future and her dreams are likely ruined. Asagai gets her more angry by arguing that her dream and her means for achieving it are inextricably bound up in the death of her father and Walter's financial savvy. While Beneatha considers herself to be independent, Asagai argues that she has been anything but.

Asagai goes on to describe his dream: he wishes to return to Nigeria, bring back what he has learned, and share it with the people of his homeland so to improve their lives. In other words, Asagai believes in bringing modern advancements from Western society back to Africa to improve the quality of life there. He is optimistic about his dream while understanding the difficulties that lie ahead. This exchange also allows Asagai to ask Beneatha to marry him and return to Africa with him in a few years. He will teach and lead the people, he says, and she can practice medicine and help take care of people. While Beneatha hesitates a bit when she says that she will consider going with him, it seems she will undoubtedly take him up on his offer. Asagai and his dream enable Beneatha to discover a new energy and shape a new dream for herself.

QUOTATIONS

4. MAMA: There is always something left to love. And if you
ain't learned that, you ain't learned nothing.

Mama makes this comment to Beneatha in Act III, near the end of
the play, as Beneatha expresses her disappointment in Walter for
losing the money in the liquor store venture and also for apparently having decided to give in to Mr. Lindner. Mama tells Beneatha
that Walter needs her to be supportive. She also says that instead of
constantly crying about herself, Beneatha should cry for Walter and
everything that he has been through and try to understand how hard
he has been trying to make everything better for his family.

One can argue that Mama speaks these words not only to Beneatha but also to the audience. Along the lines of this interpreta-
tion, she seems to be saying that if the audience hasn't learned to
love, then it hasn't learned anything yet from the play. Since the
audience when *A Raisin in the Sun* premiered in 1959 would have
been entirely or almost entirely white, we can see Mama as a powerful voice for social change.

QUOTATIONS

5. WALTER: [W]e have decided to move into our house because my father—my father—he earned it for us brick by brick. We don't want to make no trouble for nobody or fight no causes, and we will try to be good neighbors. And that's all we got to say about that. We don't want your money.

Walter delivers these words to Mr. Lindner in Act III after learning that his investment in the liquor store has been stolen. The other family members strongly disagree with Walter's decision to accept Mr. Lindner's buyout, but Walter, standing firm, decides that he will take control of the situation. Walter's refusal here comes as something of a surprise, since it requires him to shift his priorities. Whereas earlier his desire for money trumps others' needs, he now focuses all of his energy on family. Walter has finally stood up to his worries, has overcome his obsession with money and his equating of money with success, and has decided to stand by his family. We are told by the stage directions that Mama nods, eyes closed, as if she were hearing a great sermon in church. Beneatha and Ruth are finally proud of Walter, and everyone believes that Walter now has finally become a man. The Youngers will no longer defer their dreams. Instead, they will face the future as Walter does Mr. Lindner—directly and strongly, without blinking.

KEY FACTS

FULL TITLE
  A Raisin in the Sun

AUTHOR
  Lorraine Hansberry

TYPE OF WORK
  Play

GENRE
  Realist drama

LANGUAGE
  English

TIME AND PLACE WRITTEN
  1950s, New York

DATE OF FIRST PERFORMANCE
  1959

DATE OF FIRST PUBLICATION
  1959

PUBLISHER
  Random House

TONE
  Realistic

SETTING (TIME)
  Between 1945 and 1959

SETTING (PLACE)
  The South Side of Chicago

PROTAGONIST
  Walter Lee Younger

MAJOR CONFLICT
  The Youngers, a working-class black family, struggle against
  economic hardship and racial prejudice.

RISING ACTION

Ruth discovers that she is pregnant; Mama makes a down payment on a house; Mama gives Walter the remaining insurance money; Walter invests the money in the liquor store venture.

CLIMAX

Bobo tells the Youngers that Willy has run off with all of Walter's invested insurance money; Asagai makes Beneatha realize that she is not as independent as she thinks.

FALLING ACTION

Walter refuses Mr. Lindner's offer to not move; the Youngers move out of the apartment to their new house in the white neighborhood; Beneatha finds new strength in Asagai.

THEMES

The value and purpose of dreams, the need to fight racial discrimination, the importance of family

MOTIFS

Racial identity, the home

SYMBOLS

"Eat your eggs," Mama's plant, Beneatha's hair

FORESHADOWING

Mrs. Johnson's news that a black family's house has been bombed foreshadows the objections that the Clybourne Park Improvement Association will raise to the idea of the Youngers moving in; Walter's hints to Travis that he is investing the insurance money foreshadow the disappearance of the money.

STUDY QUESTIONS

1. *What are the dreams of the main characters—Mama,*
   Ruth, Beneatha, and Walter—and how are they
   deferred?

Mama dreams of moving her family out of the ghetto and into a house with a yard where children can play and she can tend a garden. Her dream has been deferred since she and her husband moved into the apartment that the Youngers still inhabit. Every day, her dream provides her with an incentive to make money. But no matter how much she and her husband strived, they could not scrape together enough money to make their dream a reality. His death and the resulting insurance money present Mama's first opportunity to realize her dream.

Ruth's dream is similar to Mama's. She wants to build a happy family and believes one step toward this goal is to own a bigger and better place to live. Ruth's dream is also deferred by a lack of money, which forces her and Walter to live in a crowded apartment where their son, Travis, must sleep on a sofa.

Beneatha's dream is to become a doctor and to save her race from ignorance. The first part of her dream may be deferred because of the money Walter loses. Her dream is also one deferred for all women. Beneatha lives in a time when society expects women to build homes rather than careers. As for saving her race from ignorance, Beneatha believes she can make people understand through action, but the exact course she chooses remains unclear at the end of the play.

Walter dreams of becoming wealthy and providing for his family as the rich people he drives around do. He often frames this dream in terms of his family—he wants to give them what he has never had. He feels like a slave to his family's economic hardship. His dream has been deferred by his poverty and inability to find decent employment. He attributes his lack of job prospects to racism, a claim that may be partially true but that is also a crutch. Over the course of the play, his understanding of his dream of gaining material wealth evolves, and by play's end, it is no longer his top priority.

2.   *What does Mama's plant represent, and how does the symbol evolve over the course of the play?*

Mama's plant, which is weak but resilient, represents her dream of living in a bigger house with a lawn. As she tends to her plant, she symbolically shows her dedication to her dream. Mama first pulls out her plant early in the morning. In fact, it is the first thing that she does in the morning; thus, at the beginning of the play we see that her plant—and her dream—are of the highest importance to her. Mama admits that the plant has never had enough sunshine but still survives. In other words, her dream has always been deferred but still remains strong. At the end of the play, Mama decides to bring the plant with her to their new home. In doing so, she gives a new significance to the plant. While it initially stands for her deferred dream, now, as her dream comes true, it reminds her of her strength in working and waiting for so many years.

3. *How does the description of the Youngers' apartment contribute to the mood of the play?*

Because all of the action of the play takes place between its walls, the Youngers' apartment determines the play's entire atmosphere and feel. The residence is very small, with one window, and the Youngers—especially Walter—feel trapped within their lives, their ghetto, and their poverty. Hansberry creates a stage that helps to illustrate this feeling of entrapment. The lack of natural light in the apartment contributes to the sense of confinement, and the tiny amount of light that does manage to trickle into the apartment is a reminder both of the Youngers' dreams and of the deferment of those dreams. Similarly, the furniture, originally chosen with pride but now old and worn, symbolizes the family itself. The Youngers are overworked and tired, and their dreams are trampled under the conditions of day-to-day existence, though they retain a core of pride that can never be entirely hidden.

How to Write
Literary Analysis

The Literary Essay: A Step-by-Step Guide

When you read for pleasure, your only goal is enjoyment. You might find yourself reading to get caught up in an exciting story, to learn about an interesting time or place, or just to pass time. Maybe you're looking for inspiration, guidance, or a reflection of your own life. There are as many different, valid ways of reading a book as there are books in the world.

When you read a work of literature in an English class, however, you're being asked to read in a special way: you're being asked to perform *literary analysis*. To analyze something means to break it down into smaller parts and then examine how those parts work, both individually and together. Literary analysis involves examining all the parts of a novel, play, short story, or poem—elements such as character, setting, tone, and imagery—and thinking about how the author uses those elements to create certain effects.

A literary essay isn't a book review: you're not being asked whether or not you liked a book or whether you'd recommend it to another reader. A literary essay also isn't like the kind of book report you wrote when you were younger, where your teacher wanted you to summarize the book's action. A high school- or college-level literary essay asks, "How does this piece of literature actually work?" "How does it do what it does?" and, "Why might the author have made the choices he or she did?"

The Seven Steps
No one is born knowing how to analyze literature; it's a skill you learn and a process you can master. As you gain more practice with this kind of thinking and writing, you'll be able to craft a method that works best for you. But until then, here are seven basic steps to writing a well-constructed literary essay:

    1. Ask questions
    2. Collect evidence
    3. Construct a thesis

4. Develop and organize arguments
5. Write the introduction
6. Write the body paragraphs
7. Write the conclusion

---

1. ASK QUESTIONS

When you're assigned a literary essay in class, your teacher will often provide you with a list of writing prompts. Lucky you! Now all you have to do is choose one. Do yourself a favor and pick a topic that interests you. You'll have a much better (not to mention easier) time if you start off with something you enjoy thinking about. If you are asked to come up with a topic by yourself, though, you might start to feel a little panicked. Maybe you have too many ideas—or none at all. Don't worry. Take a deep breath and start by asking yourself these questions:

- **What struck you?** Did a particular image, line, or scene linger in your mind for a long time? If it fascinated you, chances are you can draw on it to write a fascinating essay.

- **What confused you?** Maybe you were surprised to see a character act in a certain way, or maybe you didn't understand why the book ended the way it did. Confusing moments in a work of literature are like a loose thread in a sweater: if you pull on it, you can unravel the entire thing. Ask yourself why the author chose to write about that character or scene the way he or she did and you might tap into some important insights about the work as a whole.

- **Did you notice any patterns?** Is there a phrase that the main character uses constantly or an image that repeats throughout the book? If you can figure out how that pattern weaves through the work and what the significance of that pattern is, you've almost got your entire essay mapped out.

- **Did you notice any contradictions or ironies?** Great works of literature are complex; great literary essays recognize and explain those complexities. Maybe the title (*Happy Days*) totally disagrees with the book's subject matter (hungry orphans dying in the woods). Maybe the main character acts one way around his family and a completely different way around his friends and associates. If you can find a way to explain a work's contradictory elements, you've got the seeds of a great essay.

At this point, you don't need to know exactly what you're going to say about your topic; you just need a place to begin your exploration. You can help direct your reading and brainstorming by formulating your topic as a *question,* which you'll then try to answer in your essay. The best questions invite critical debates and discussions, not just a rehashing of the summary. Remember, you're looking for something you can *prove or argue* based on evidence you find in the text. Finally, remember to keep the scope of your question in mind: is this a topic you can adequately address within the word or page limit you've been given? Conversely, is this a topic big enough to fill the required length?

GOOD QUESTIONS

> *"Are Romeo and Juliet's parents responsible for the deaths of their children?"*
> *"Why do pigs keep showing up in* LORD OF THE FLIES?*"*
> *"Are Dr. Frankenstein and his monster alike? How?"*

BAD QUESTIONS

> *"What happens to Scout in* TO KILL A MOCKINGBIRD?*"*
> *"What do the other characters in* JULIUS CAESAR *think about Caesar?"*
> *"How does Hester Prynne in* THE SCARLET LETTER *remind me of my sister?"*

---

2. COLLECT EVIDENCE

Once you know what question you want to answer, it's time to scour the book for things that will help you answer the question. Don't worry if you don't know what you want to say yet—right now you're just collecting ideas and material and letting it all percolate. Keep track of passages, symbols, images, or scenes that deal with your topic. Eventually, you'll start making connections between these examples and your thesis will emerge.

Here's a brief summary of the various parts that compose each and every work of literature. These are the elements that you will analyze in your essay, and which you will offer as evidence to support your arguments. For more on the parts of literary works, see the Glossary of Literary Terms at the end of this section.

ELEMENTS OF STORY   These are the *what*s of the work—what happens, where it happens, and to whom it happens.

- **Plot:** All of the events and actions of the work.
- **Character:** The people who act and are acted upon in a literary work. The main character of a work is known as the *protagonist.*
- **Conflict:** The central tension in the work. In most cases, the protagonist wants something, while opposing forces (antagonists) hinder the protagonist's progress.
- **Setting:** When and where the work takes place. Elements of setting include location, time period, time of day, weather, social atmosphere, and economic conditions.
- **Narrator:** The person telling the story. The narrator may straightforwardly report what happens, convey the subjective opinions and perceptions of one or more characters, or provide commentary and opinion in his or her own voice.
- **Themes:** The main idea or message of the work—usually an abstract idea about people, society, or life in general. A work may have many themes, which may be in tension with one another.

ELEMENTS OF STYLE   These are the *how*s—how the characters speak, how the story is constructed, and how language is used throughout the work.

- **Structure and organization:** How the parts of the work are assembled. Some novels are narrated in a linear, chronological fashion, while others skip around in time. Some plays follow a traditional three- or five-act structure, while others are a series of loosely connected scenes. Some authors deliberately leave gaps in their works, leaving readers to puzzle out the missing information. A work's structure and organization can tell you a lot about the kind of message it wants to convey.
- **Point of view:** The perspective from which a story is told. In *first-person point of view,* the narrator involves him or herself in the story. ("I went to the store"; "We watched in horror as the bird slammed into the window.") A first-person narrator is usually the protagonist of the work, but not always. In *third-person point of view,* the narrator does not participate

in the story. A third-person narrator may closely follow a specific character, recounting that individual character's thoughts or experiences, or it may be what we call an *omniscient* narrator. Omniscient narrators see and know all: they can witness any event in any time or place and are privy to the inner thoughts and feelings of all characters. Remember that the narrator and the author are not the same thing!

- **Diction:** Word choice. Whether a character uses dry, clinical language or flowery prose with lots of exclamation points can tell you a lot about his or her attitude and personality.

- **Syntax:** Word order and sentence construction. Syntax is a crucial part of establishing an author's narrative voice. Ernest Hemingway, for example, is known for writing in very short, straightforward sentences, while James Joyce characteristically wrote in long, incredibly complicated lines.

- **Tone:** The mood or feeling of the text. Diction and syntax often contribute to the tone of a work. A novel written in short, clipped sentences that use small, simple words might feel brusque, cold, or matter-of-fact.

- **Imagery:** Language that appeals to the senses, representing things that can be seen, smelled, heard, tasted, or touched.

- **Figurative language:** Language that is not meant to be interpreted literally. The most common types of figurative language are *metaphors* and *similes,* which compare two unlike things in order to suggest a similarity between them— for example, "All the world's a stage," or "The moon is like a ball of green cheese." (Metaphors say one thing *is* another thing; similes claim that one thing is *like* another thing.)

---

3. Construct a Thesis

When you've examined all the evidence you've collected and know how you want to answer the question, it's time to write your thesis statement. A *thesis* is a claim about a work of literature that needs to be supported by evidence and arguments. The thesis statement is the heart of the literary essay, and the bulk of your paper will be spent trying to prove this claim. A good thesis will be:

- **Arguable.** "*The Great Gatsby* describes New York society in the 1920s" isn't a thesis—it's a fact.

- **Provable through textual evidence**. "*Hamlet* is a confusing but ultimately very well-written play" is a weak thesis because it offers the writer's personal opinion about the book. Yes, it's arguable, but it's not a claim that can be proved or supported with examples taken from the play itself.

- **Surprising**. "Both George and Lenny change a great deal in *Of Mice and Men*" is a weak thesis because it's obvious. A really strong thesis will argue for a reading of the text that is not immediately apparent.

- **Specific**. "Dr. Frankenstein's monster tells us a lot about the human condition" is *almost* a really great thesis statement, but it's still too vague. What does the writer mean by "a lot"? *How* does the monster tell us so much about the human condition?

GOOD THESIS STATEMENTS

Question: In *Romeo and Juliet*, which is more powerful in shaping the lovers' story: fate or foolishness?

Thesis: "Though Shakespeare defines Romeo and Juliet as 'star-crossed lovers' and images of stars and planets appear throughout the play, a closer examination of that celestial imagery reveals that the stars are merely witnesses to the characters' foolish activities and not the causes themselves."

Question: How does the bell jar function as a symbol in Sylvia Plath's *The Bell Jar*?

Thesis: "A bell jar is a bell-shaped glass that has three basic uses: to hold a specimen for observation, to contain gases, and to maintain a vacuum. The bell jar appears in each of these capacities in *The Bell Jar*, Plath's semi-autobiographical novel, and each appearance marks a different stage in Esther's mental breakdown."

Question: Would Piggy in *The Lord of the Flies* make a good island leader if he were given the chance?

Thesis: "Though the intelligent, rational, and innovative Piggy has the mental characteristics of a good leader, he ultimately lacks the social skills necessary to be an effective one. Golding emphasizes this point by giving Piggy a foil in the charismatic Jack, whose magnetic personality allows him to capture and wield power effectively, if not always wisely."

4. DEVELOP AND ORGANIZE ARGUMENTS

The reasons and examples that support your thesis will form the middle paragraphs of your essay. Since you can't really write your thesis statement until you know how you'll structure your argument, you'll probably end up working on steps 3 and 4 at the same time.

There's no single method of argumentation that will work in every context. One essay prompt might ask you to compare and contrast two characters, while another asks you to trace an image through a given work of literature. These questions require different kinds of answers and therefore different kinds of arguments. Below, we'll discuss three common kinds of essay prompts and some strategies for constructing a solid, well-argued case.

TYPES OF LITERARY ESSAYS

- **Compare and contrast**

    Compare and contrast the characters of Huck and Jim in THE ADVENTURES OF HUCKLEBERRY FINN.

    Chances are you've written this kind of essay before. In an academic literary context, you'll organize your arguments the same way you would in any other class. You can either go *subject by subject* or *point by point*. In the former, you'll discuss one character first and then the second. In the latter, you'll choose several traits (attitude toward life, social status, images and metaphors associated with the character) and devote a paragraph to each. You may want to use a mix of these two approaches—for example, you may want to spend a paragraph apiece broadly sketching Huck's and Jim's personalities before transitioning into a paragraph or two that describes a few key points of comparison. This can be a highly effective strategy if you want to make a counterintuitive argument—that, despite seeming to be totally different, the two objects being compared are actually similar in a very important way (or vice versa). Remember that your essay should reveal something fresh or unexpected about the text, so think beyond the obvious parallels and differences.

- **Trace**

    Choose an image—for example, birds, knives, or eyes—and trace that image throughout MACBETH.

    Sounds pretty easy, right? All you need to do is read the play, underline every appearance of a knife in *Macbeth,* and then list them in your essay in the order they appear, right? Well, not exactly. Your teacher doesn't want a simple catalog of examples. He or she wants to see you make *connections* between those examples—that's the difference between summarizing and analyzing. In the *Macbeth* example above, think about the different contexts in which knives appear in the play and to what effect. In *Macbeth,* there are real knives and imagined knives; knives that kill and knives that simply threaten. Categorize and classify your examples to give them some order. Finally, always keep the overall effect in mind. After you choose and analyze your examples, you should come to some greater understanding about the work, as well as your chosen image, symbol, or phrase's role in developing the major themes and stylistic strategies of that work.

- **Debate**

  Is the society depicted in 1984 *good for its citizens?*

  In this kind of essay, you're being asked to debate a moral, ethical, or aesthetic issue regarding the work. You might be asked to judge a character or group of characters (*Is Caesar responsible for his own demise?*) or the work itself (*Is* JANE EYRE *a feminist novel?*). For this kind of essay, there are two important points to keep in mind. First, don't simply base your arguments on your personal feelings and reactions. Every literary essay expects you to read and analyze the work, so search for evidence in the text. What do characters in *1984* have to say about the government of Oceania? What images does Orwell use that might give you a hint about his attitude toward the government? As in any debate, you also need to make sure that you define all the necessary terms before you begin to argue your case. What does it mean to be a "good" society? What makes a novel "feminist"? You should define your terms right up front, in the first paragraph after your introduction.

  Second, remember that strong literary essays make contrary and surprising arguments. Try to think outside the box. In the *1984* example above, it seems like the obvious answer would be no, the totalitarian society depicted in Orwell's novel is *not* good for its citizens. But can you think of any arguments for the opposite side? Even if your final assertion is that the novel depicts a cruel, repressive, and therefore harmful society, acknowledging and responding to the counterargument will strengthen your overall case.

5. WRITE THE INTRODUCTION

Your introduction sets up the entire essay. It's where you present your topic and articulate the particular issues and questions you'll be addressing. It's also where you, as the writer, introduce yourself to your readers. A persuasive literary essay immediately establishes its writer as a knowledgeable, authoritative figure.

An introduction can vary in length depending on the overall length of the essay, but in a traditional five-paragraph essay it should be no longer than one paragraph. However long it is, your introduction needs to:

- **Provide any necessary context.** Your introduction should situate the reader and let him or her know what to expect. What book are you discussing? Which characters? What topic will you be addressing?

- **Answer the "So what?" question.** Why is this topic important, and why is your particular position on the topic noteworthy? Ideally, your introduction should pique the reader's interest by suggesting how your argument is surprising or otherwise counterintuitive. Literary essays make unexpected connections and reveal less-than-obvious truths.

- **Present your thesis.** This usually happens at or very near the end of your introduction.

- **Indicate the shape of the essay to come.** Your reader should finish reading your introduction with a good sense of the scope of your essay as well as the path you'll take toward proving your thesis. You don't need to spell out every step, but you do need to suggest the organizational pattern you'll be using.

Your introduction should not:

- **Be vague.** Beware of the two killer words in literary analysis: *interesting* and *important*. Of course the work, question, or example is interesting and important—that's why you're writing about it!

- **Open with any grandiose assertions.** Many student readers think that beginning their essays with a flamboyant statement such as, "Since the dawn of time, writers have been fascinated with the topic of free will," makes them sound important and commanding. You know what? It actually sounds pretty amateurish.

- **Wildly praise the work.** Another typical mistake student writers make is extolling the work or author. Your teacher doesn't need to be told that "Shakespeare is perhaps the greatest writer in the English language." You can mention a work's reputation in passing—by referring to *The Adventures of Huckleberry Finn* as "Mark Twain's enduring classic," for example—but don't make a point of bringing it up unless that reputation is key to your argument.

- **Go off-topic.** Keep your introduction streamlined and to the point. Don't feel the need to throw in all kinds of bells and whistles in order to impress your reader—just get to the point as quickly as you can, without skimping on any of the required steps.

---

6. WRITE THE BODY PARAGRAPHS

Once you've written your introduction, you'll take the arguments you developed in step 4 and turn them into your body paragraphs. The organization of this middle section of your essay will largely be determined by the argumentative strategy you use, but no matter how you arrange your thoughts, your body paragraphs need to do the following:

- **Begin with a strong topic sentence.** Topic sentences are like signs on a highway: they tell the reader where they are and where they're going. A good topic sentence not only alerts readers to what issue will be discussed in the following paragraph but also gives them a sense of what argument will be made *about* that issue. "Rumor and gossip play an important role in *The Crucible*" isn't a strong topic sentence because it doesn't tell us very much. "The community's constant gossiping creates an environment that allows false accusations to flourish" is a much stronger topic sentence— it not only tells us *what* the paragraph will discuss (gossip) but *how* the paragraph will discuss the topic (by showing how gossip creates a set of conditions that leads to the play's climactic action).

- **Fully and completely develop a single thought.** Don't skip around in your paragraph or try to stuff in too much material. Body paragraphs are like bricks: each individual one needs to be strong and sturdy or the entire structure will collapse. Make sure you have really proven your point before moving on to the next one.

- **Use transitions effectively.** Good literary essay writers know that each paragraph must be clearly and strongly linked to the material around it. Think of each paragraph as a response to the one that precedes it. Use transition words and phrases such as *however, similarly, on the contrary, therefore,* and *furthermore* to indicate what kind of response you're making.

---

7. WRITE THE CONCLUSION

Just as you used the introduction to ground your readers in the topic before providing your thesis, you'll use the conclusion to quickly summarize the specifics learned thus far and then hint at the broader implications of your topic. A good conclusion will:

- **Do more than simply restate the thesis.** If your thesis argued that *The Catcher in the Rye* can be read as a Christian allegory, don't simply end your essay by saying, "And that is why *The Catcher in the Rye* can be read as a Christian allegory." If you've constructed your arguments well, this kind of statement will just be redundant.

- **Synthesize the arguments, not summarize them.** Similarly, don't repeat the details of your body paragraphs in your conclusion. The reader has already read your essay, and chances are it's not so long that they've forgotten all your points by now.

- **Revisit the "So what?" question.** In your introduction, you made a case for why your topic and position are important. You should close your essay with the same sort of gesture. What do your readers know now that they didn't know before? How will that knowledge help them better appreciate or understand the work overall?

- **Move from the specific to the general.** Your essay has most likely treated a very specific element of the work—a single character, a small set of images, or a particular passage. In your conclusion, try to show how this narrow discussion has wider implications for the work overall. If your essay on *To Kill a Mockingbird* focused on the character of Boo Radley, for example, you might want to include a bit in your conclusion about how he fits into the novel's larger message about childhood, innocence, or family life.

- **Stay relevant.** Your conclusion should suggest new directions of thought, but it shouldn't be treated as an opportunity to pad your essay with all the extra, interesting ideas you came up with during your brainstorming sessions but couldn't fit into the essay proper. Don't attempt to stuff in unrelated queries or too many abstract thoughts.

- **Avoid making overblown closing statements.** A conclusion should open up your highly specific, focused discussion, but it should do so without drawing a sweeping lesson about life or human nature. Making such observations may be part of the point of reading, but it's almost always a mistake in essays, where these observations tend to sound overly dramatic or simply silly.

A+ Essay Checklist

Congratulations! If you've followed all the steps we've outlined above, you should have a solid literary essay to show for all your efforts. What if you've got your sights set on an A+? To write the kind of superlative essay that will be rewarded with a perfect grade, keep the following rubric in mind. These are the qualities that teachers expect to see in a truly A+ essay. How does yours stack up?

- ✓ Demonstrates a thorough understanding of the book
- ✓ Presents an original, compelling argument
- ✓ Thoughtfully analyzes the text's formal elements
- ✓ Uses appropriate and insightful examples
- ✓ Structures ideas in a logical and progressive order
- ✓ Demonstrates a mastery of sentence construction, transitions, grammar, spelling, and word choice

Suggested Essay Topics

1. *How does the idea of assimilationism become important?*

2. *Discuss the title of the play. How does it relate to the dreams of each of the characters?*

3. *How do power and authority change hands over the course of the play?*

4. *Discuss how minor characters such as George Murchison, Willy Harris, and Mr. Lindner represent the ideas against which the main characters react.*

5. *What sort of statement does Hansberry seem to be making about race? Does she make more than one statement? If so, do these statements conflict with each other?*

A+ STUDENT ESSAY

What role does money play in *A Raisin in the Sun*?

For several of Hansberry's characters, money is a promise of salvation, a gift to be stored up and fought for whenever possible. But as the story unfolds, the Younger family must repeatedly weigh their wish for material wealth against their wish for freedom. Beneatha, Walter, and the others ultimately choose abstract ideals—education, dignity, love—over easy alternatives that hold out the promise of more money. By dramatizing the crises they face before they arrive at these decisions, Hansberry shows that wealth is not always as desirable as it seems, and she reminds us of the sacrifices people make for their freedom.

Throughout the play, members of the Younger family act as if money is too precious to be parted with. In the opening scene, Travis asks his mother for fifty cents, and the seemingly paltry sum is too much for the impoverished Ruth Younger to give away. Although Beneatha doesn't love George Murchison, her family tells her to continue dating him and taking pride in the match, because George comes from a wealthy family. A financial offer from the Clybourne Welcoming Committee briefly seduces Walter: The money would give him an opportunity to start his own business and become rich. Ruth considers an abortion because her unborn child would drain the Youngers of the little money they currently have. Walter pleads with his mother to donate her ten thousand dollars to his liquor-store scheme, arguing that the Youngers would benefit from the liquor sales. Almost every character shows an occasional lust for money.

However, each time the Youngers are presented with an opportunity to gain or save their money, they must relinquish something else that is valuable. If Mama doesn't give Travis the fifty cents he asks for, she denies him the chance to participate in a classroom activity, furthering his education and bolstering his pride. By settling for the wealthy George, Beneatha would sacrifice her intellectual passion and spend the rest of her life with a man who casually admits to disliking books. Accepting the offer from the Clybourne Welcoming Committee would mean capitulating to a racist demand: The whites have offered the money to the Youngers because the whites do not want to live in an interracial community. As Mama argues,

Ruth's money-saving abortion would represent a moral defeat for the Youngers, an acknowledgment that the family does not have the love and energy to support a new person. Money that assists Walter in his liquor store plans could instead be invested in Beneatha's education or a house for Travis—less lucrative ideals that Mama nonetheless clearly prefers to Walter's dream. Nowhere in *A Raisin in the Sun* does a character guiltlessly accept or hold onto his or her money.

Again and again, the rejection of wealth is a cause for celebration among Hansberry's characters. Ruth laughs when Walter gives his fifty cents to Travis; the couple acknowledges that the act of generosity is the right decision. Mama does not argue with Beneatha when she announces her rejection of George, and Beneatha comments on this rare instance of maternal understanding. The climax of the play occurs when Walter rejects the offer from the Welcoming Committee; both Mama and Ruth declare their pride in this deeply flawed man. Ruth chooses not to have an abortion, to Mama's great relief. The investment in a house for Travis delights each of the Youngers except Walter, and even Walter eventually recognizes the dignity and wisdom behind this hard decision. Each time a character turns down an easy financial offer, the other characters applaud his farsightedness and strength.

It's surprising that money turns out to be a villain in the Younger family's story. Like Ruth and Walter, we initially think that any offer of cash is a blessing for the Youngers because it represents a chance to abandon their dingy apartment and begin a new life. But Hansberry shows that no price is high enough for freedom. The black characters she describes must defend their right to an education, a loving home, and a sense of self-worth—even when the white community wants to pay them to abandon these ideals. Throughout the play, Hansberry conveys a sense of anger and disgust. No family should have to make the choices that confront the Youngers as their dreams are repeatedly deferred.

LITERARY ANALYSIS

GLOSSARY OF LITERARY TERMS

ANTAGONIST

The entity that acts to frustrate the goals of the *protagonist*. The antagonist is usually another *character* but may also be a non-human force.

ANTIHERO / ANTIHEROINE

A *protagonist* who is not admirable or who challenges notions of what should be considered admirable.

CHARACTER

A person, animal, or any other thing with a personality that appears in a *narrative*.

CLIMAX

The moment of greatest intensity in a text or the major turning point in the *plot*.

CONFLICT

The central struggle that moves the *plot* forward. The conflict can be the *protagonist*'s struggle against fate, nature, society, or another person.

FIRST-PERSON POINT OF VIEW

A literary style in which the *narrator* tells the story from his or her own *point of view* and refers to himself or herself as "I." The narrator may be an active participant in the story or just an observer.

HERO / HEROINE

The principal *character* in a literary work or *narrative*.

IMAGERY

Language that brings to mind sense-impressions, representing things that can be seen, smelled, heard, tasted, or touched.

MOTIF

A recurring idea, structure, contrast, or device that develops or informs the major *themes* of a work of literature.

NARRATIVE

A story.

NARRATOR

The person (sometimes a *character*) who tells a story; the *voice* assumed by the writer. The narrator and the author of the work of literature are not the same person.

PLOT

The arrangement of the events in a story, including the sequence in which they are told, the relative emphasis they are given, and the causal connections between events.

POINT OF VIEW

The *perspective* that a *narrative* takes toward the events it describes.

PROTAGONIST

The main *character* around whom the story revolves.

SETTING

The location of a *narrative* in time and space. Setting creates mood or atmosphere.

SUBPLOT

A secondary *plot* that is of less importance to the overall story but may serve as a point of contrast or comparison to the main plot.

SYMBOL

An object, *character,* figure, or color that is used to represent an abstract idea or concept. Unlike an *emblem,* a symbol may have different meanings in different contexts.

SYNTAX

The way the words in a piece of writing are put together to form lines, phrases, or clauses; the basic structure of a piece of writing.

THEME

A fundamental and universal idea explored in a literary work.

TONE

The author's attitude toward the subject or *characters* of a story or poem or toward the reader.

VOICE

An author's individual way of using language to reflect his or her own personality and attitudes. An author communicates voice through *tone, diction,* and *syntax.*

LITERARY ANALYSIS

A NOTE ON PLAGIARISM

Plagiarism—presenting someone else's work as your own—rears its ugly head in many forms. Many students know that copying text without citing it is unacceptable. But some don't realize that even if you're not quoting directly, but instead are paraphrasing or summarizing, *it is plagiarism* unless you cite the source.

Here are the most common forms of plagiarism:

- Using an author's phrases, sentences, or paragraphs without citing the source
- Paraphrasing an author's ideas without citing the source
- Passing off another student's work as your own

How do you steer clear of plagiarism? You should *always* acknowledge all words and ideas that aren't your own by using quotation marks around verbatim text or citations like footnotes and endnotes to note another writer's ideas. For more information on how to give credit when credit is due, ask your teacher for guidance or visit www.sparknotes.com.

Review & Resources

Quiz

1. In what city do the Youngers live?

   A. New York City
   B. Los Angeles
   C. St. Louis
   D. Chicago

2. From whom are the Youngers awaiting a check?

   A. An insurance company
   B. A distant relative
   C. Walter's employer
   D. The government

3. What does Ruth find out when she goes to the doctor?

   A. That she has asthma
   B. That she is overtired
   C. That her fainting spells are nothing to worry about
   D. That she is pregnant

4. What does Walter's employer call to say?

   A. That Walter is getting a raise
   B. That Walter must come in earlier
   C. That Walter has not been to work in three days
   D. That Walter cannot have the vacation they discussed

5. What do the Youngers give Mama on the day they move?

   A. A new coat
   B. Gardening equipment
   C. New curtains
   D. A plant

6. What does Beneatha want to be?

    A. A lawyer
    B. A doctor
    C. A teacher
    D. An actress

7. What does Karl Lindner want the Youngers to do?

    A. Join the Clybourne Park Improvement Association
    B. Work in the community garden
    C. Give up moving to Clybourne Park
    D. Invest in a liquor store

8. Which country does Joseph Asagai come from?

    A. Nigeria
    B. Ethiopia
    C. Tanzania
    D. Liberia

9. When he is fooling around with Beneatha, what does Walter call himself?

    A. Bronze Arrow
    B. Flaming Spear
    C. Thunder and Lightning
    D. The King

10. Who is the Youngers' next-door neighbor?

    A. Mrs. Jones
    B. Mrs. Lindner
    C. Mrs. Darrow
    D. Mrs. Johnson

11. Where does Mama keep her plant?

    A. In her bedroom
    B. In the bathroom
    C. Outside the window
    D. In the living room

12. Where does Travis sleep?

   A. In his parents' bedroom
   B. In his own room
   C. In Beneatha's room
   D. In the living room

13. What does Ruth buy in her excitement about the Youngers' new home?

   A. Curtains
   B. A rug
   C. A new shirt for Travis
   D. A puppy

14. What does Ruth tell Walter to do when he complains incessantly about his life?

   A. Eat his words
   B. Eat his eggs
   C. Beat his boss
   D. Go outside

15. Where do Ruth and Walter go when they are becoming more hopeful about the future?

   A. To a dance
   B. To the movies
   C. To a roller rink
   D. To a bar

16. In what year was *A Raisin in the Sun* first performed?

   A. 1947
   B. 1973
   C. 1959
   D. 1962

REVIEW & RESOURCES

17. What does Ruth consider when she finds out that she is pregnant?

   A. Having an abortion
   B. Buying a maternity dress
   C. Not moving with her family
   D. Quitting her job

18. Why do Ruth and Mama approve of George Murchison?

   A. Because he dresses well
   B. Because he is handsome and wealthy
   C. Because he takes Beneatha to the theater
   D. Because he is politically active

19. Who is the last to leave the Younger apartment at the end of the play?

   A. Walter
   B. Ruth
   C. Beneatha
   D. Mama

20. Whom does Mrs. Johnson quote when she visits the Youngers' apartment?

   A. Mr. Johnson
   B. Booker T. Washington
   C. Malcolm X
   D. Martin Luther King, Jr.

21. At what point does Mama say that Walter has finally achieved his "manhood"?

   A. When he invests in the liquor store
   B. When he takes Ruth out to dinner
   C. When she finds out that Ruth is pregnant
   D. When he tells Mr. Lindner that they will move to Clybourne Park no matter what

22. What happens to the money that Walter invests in the liquor store?

    A.   Willy Harris runs off with it

    B.   It is used to bribe members of the government

    C.   It is used for the first month's rent on the store space

    D.   Mr. Lindner puts it in the bank for the Youngers

23. Near the end of the play, what does Asagai leave Beneatha to think about?

    A.   Her anatomy test

    B.   Whether she wants to be an assimilationist

    C.   Whether she will marry him and move to Africa

    D.   Whether straightening her hair is "mutilation"

24. What does Travis do to make money?

    A.   He begs on the street

    B.   He carries bags at the grocery store

    C.   He has a paper route

    D.   He does chores around their apartment

25. Where does Walter often go to escape the apartment?

    A.   To a bar

    B.   To a pool hall

    C.   To the movies

    D.   To the dance hall

Suggestions for Further Reading

CARTER, STEVEN R. *Hansberry's Drama: Commitment Amid Complexity.* Urbana: University of Illinois Press, 1991.

CHENEY, ANNE. *Lorraine Hansberry.* Boston: Twayne, 1984.

DOMINA, LYNN. *Understanding* A RAISIN IN THE SUN: *A Student's Casebook to Issues, Sources, and Historical Documents.* Westport: Greenwood Press, 1998.

HALBERSTAM, DAVID. *The Fifties.* New York: Villard Books, 1993.

HUGHES, LANGSTON. *Selected Poems of Langston Hughes.* New York: Vintage Books, 1990.

MAY, ELAINE TYLER. *Homeward Bound: American Families in the Cold War Era.* New York: Basic Books, 1988.

MEYEROWITZ, JOANNE, ed. *Not June Cleaver: Women and Gender in Postwar America, 1945–1960.* Philadelphia: Temple University Press, 1994.

NEMIROFF, ROBERT, ed. *To Be Young, Gifted, and Black: Lorraine Hansberry in Her Own Words.* With an introduction by James Baldwin. Englewood Cliffs, New Jersey: Prentice-Hall, 1969.

SMITH, JUDITH. *Visions of Belonging: Family Stories, Popular Culture, and Postwar Democracy, 1940–1960.* New York: Columbia University Press, 2004.

REVIEW & RESOURCES